Inside the NFL

Houston Texans

BY
ZACH WYNER

AV² provides enriched content that supplements and complements this book. Weigl's AV² books strive to create inspired learning and engage young minds in a total learning experience.

Your AV² Media Enhanced books come alive with...

Audio
Listen to sections of the book read aloud.

Key Words
Study vocabulary, and complete a matching word activity.

Video
Watch informative video clips.

Quizzes
Test your knowledge.

Go to **www.av2books.com**, and enter this book's unique code.

BOOK CODE

D663907

Embedded Weblinks
Gain additional information for research.

Slide Show
View images and captions, and prepare a presentation.

AV² by Weigl brings you media enhanced books that support active learning.

Try This!
Complete activities and hands-on experiments.

... and much, much more!

Published by AV² by Weigl
350 5th Avenue, 59th Floor
New York, NY 10118
Websites: www.av2books.com   www.weigl.com

Library of Congress Control Number: 2014930783

ISBN 978-1-4896-0830-7 (hardcover)
ISBN 978-1-4896-0832-1 (single-user eBook)
ISBN 978-1-4896-0833-8 (multi-user eBook)

Printed in the United States of America in North Mankato, Minnesota
1 2 3 4 5 6 7 8 9 0   18 17 16 15 14

042014
WEP150314

Project Coordinator Aaron Carr
Art Director Terry Paulhus

Photo Credits
Every reasonable effort has been made to trace ownership and to obtain permission to reprint copyright material. The publishers would be pleased to have any errors or omissions brought to their attention so that they may be corrected in subsequent printings.

Weigl acknowledges Getty Images as its primary image supplier for this title.

Houston Texans

CONTENTS

Introduction

I n 1995, the city of Houston, Texas, was stunned to learn that their Oilers, a team that had benefitted from years of unwavering support, was planning a move to Nashville, Tennessee. For 37 years, professional football had thrived in Houston. By the end of the 1996 season, the team was gone. Fans in Houston focused on college and high school football, holding out little hope that the National Football League (NFL) would award an expansion franchise to the city when major markets such as Los Angeles, California, and Toronto, Canada, were both in the running for a new team.

Houston football fans did not expect that a group of determined businessmen would make the NFL an offer they could not refuse. Suddenly, to the delight of local fans, professional football was a reality in Houston once again.

In 2002, the Houston Texans became the newest team to join the NFL. The NFL is not expected to expand again until 2015 at the earliest.

In 2002, the Houston Texans were born. When they arrived, they found a fan base ready to stand by them through their growing pains, and await their rise through the **playoffs**, to the top of the NFL.

J. J. Watt is the current starting defensive end for the Texans. He was drafted by Houston in 2011.

TEXANS

Stadium	NRG Stadium
Division	American Football Conference (AFC) South
Head coach	Wade Phillips
Location	Houston, Texas
Super Bowl titles	None
Nicknames	None

2
Playoff
Appearances

2
Playoff
Victories

2
Division
Championships

History

BACK TO BACK

The Texans' only two playoff appearances came in back-to-back seasons as the team captured the AFC South in

• **2011 and 2012** •

⊔ Mario Williams was the first overall pick by the Houston Texans in the 2006 NFL Draft.

I n October of 1999, six months after learning that they had lost the bid for the 32nd NFL team to Los Angeles, Bob McNair and the people that made up Houston NFL Holdings found out that NFL owners had reversed their decision. The 32nd NFL franchise would be awarded to Houston.

In 2001, the team named Dom Capers their first head coach. By the end of the year, the Texans signed their first 10 players. In February of 2002, the Texans drafted a grouping of players in the Expansion Draft and in August of that year, the Texans took the field. The first five seasons of any expansion franchise are rough. The Texans were no exception. Following the 2005 season, Dom Capers was relieved of his coaching duties and replaced by Gary Kubiak. The next season, Kubiak rode rising stars DeMeco Ryans, Mario Williams, Andre Johnson, and Matt Schaub to the team's first **.500 season**.

In 2011, following the team's first winning season, the Houston Texans won 10 games, the American Football Conference (AFC) South division title, and their first playoff game. The next year, they improved on their breakout season as Defensive Player of the Year J. J. Watt sparked the club to 12 wins, another AFC South title, and a playoff win against the Cincinnati Bengals.

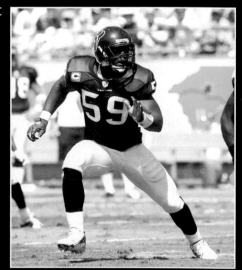

⊔ DeMeco Ryans' 155 tackles in 2006 were 31 more than the league's next closest rookie.

The Stadium

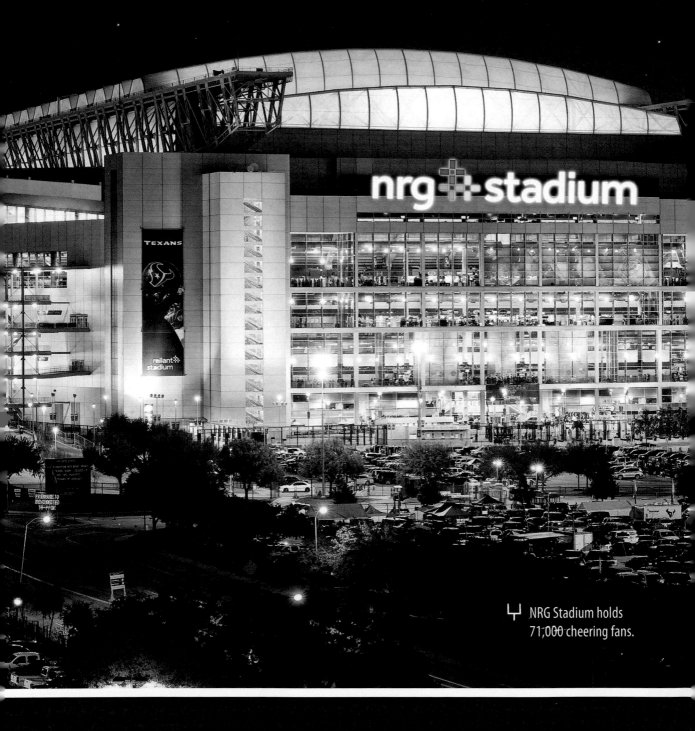

NRG Stadium holds 71,000 cheering fans.

It goes without saying that without a home there is no team, but in the case of NRG Stadium, this statement is especially true. Because the city of Houston competed with cities such as Toronto and Los Angeles for the honor of hosting an NFL franchise, they needed to show the level of their commitment to NFL officials. Plans to build the state of the art NRG Stadium were crucial in convincing NFL owners to award the 32nd NFL franchise to Houston.

Texans fans have known only one place, NRG Stadium, where the team has played all of its home games since 2002.

The very first NFL home stadium to have a **retractable roof**, NRG Stadium has a unique ability to keep its fans comfortable no matter the weather. Amazingly, the roof can be opened or closed in as little as seven minutes. While fans cheer for their beloved Texans, they can catch any plays they might have missed on one of the largest digital video screens offered by any sports venue in the world. In addition to hosting the Texans, NRG Stadium hosts the Houston Livestock Show and Rodeo, the Texas Bowl, and has been the home of both the **Super Bowl** and WrestleMania.

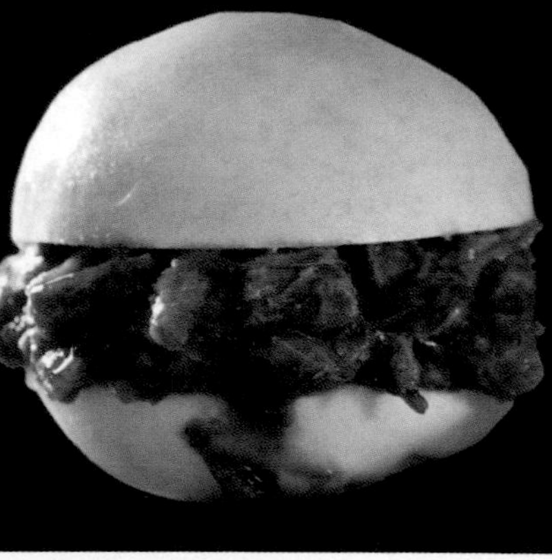

Hungry Texans fans line up for a roasted pork belly sandwich served on a bao bun with hoisin sauce and quick-pickled cucumbers.

Where They Play

CANADA

Washington · 30

Oregon

Montana

North Dakota

Minnesota · *Lake Superior*

Idaho

South Dakota

Wisconsin · 23

22

Nevada

Wyoming

14

Nebraska

Iowa · 24

13 · Illinois

29

California · 15

Utah

Colorado

Kansas

Missouri · 31

16

Arizona

New Mexico

Oklahoma

Arkansas

32

Pacific Ocean

UNITED STATES

Texas

17

Mississippi

Louisiana

12

27

Gulf of Mexico

MEXICO

Alaska

0   500 Miles
0   500 km

Hawai'i

0   100 Miles
0   100 km

AMERICAN FOOTBALL CONFERENCE

EAST		NORTH		SOUTH		WEST	
1	Gillette Stadium	5	FirstEnergy Stadium	9	EverBank Field	13	Arrowhead Stadium
2	MetLife Stadium	6	Heinz Field	10	LP Field	14	Sports Authority Field at Mile High
3	Ralph Wilson Stadium	7	M&T Bank Stadium	11	Lucas Oil Stadium	15	O.co Coliseum
4	Sun Life Stadium	8	Paul Brown Stadium	★12	NRG Stadium	16	Qualcomm Stadium

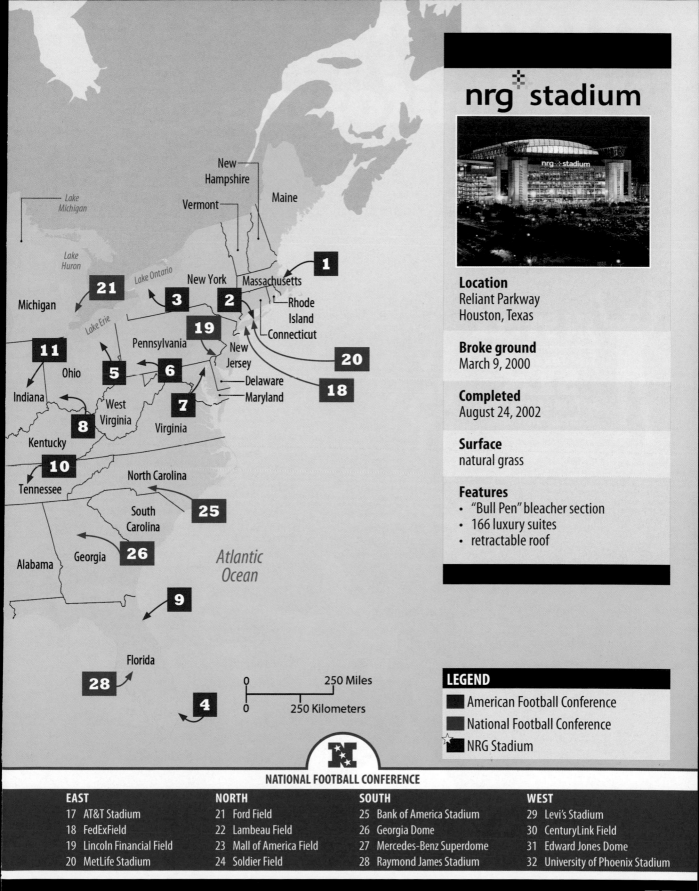

nrg stadium

Location
Reliant Parkway
Houston, Texas

Broke ground
March 9, 2000

Completed
August 24, 2002

Surface
natural grass

Features
- "Bull Pen" bleacher section
- 166 luxury suites
- retractable roof

New Hampshire
Maine
Vermont
Lake Michigan
Lake Huron
Lake Ontario
New York
Massachusetts
Rhode Island
Connecticut
Michigan
Lake Erie
Pennsylvania
New Jersey
Ohio
Delaware
Indiana
West Virginia
Maryland
Kentucky
Virginia
Tennessee
North Carolina
South Carolina
Alabama
Georgia
Atlantic Ocean
Florida

0   250 Miles
0   250 Kilometers

LEGEND
- American Football Conference
- National Football Conference
- NRG Stadium

NATIONAL FOOTBALL CONFERENCE

EAST		NORTH		SOUTH		WEST	
17	AT&T Stadium	21	Ford Field	25	Bank of America Stadium	29	Levi's Stadium
18	FedExField	22	Lambeau Field	26	Georgia Dome	30	CenturyLink Field
19	Lincoln Financial Field	23	Mall of America Field	27	Mercedes-Benz Superdome	31	Edward Jones Dome
20	MetLife Stadium	24	Soldier Field	28	Raymond James Stadium	32	University of Phoenix Stadium

The Uniforms

IN STYLE

The Texans have **SIX** different uniform combinations.

⊔ Undrafted out of college, Arian Foster has proved many NFL scouts wrong with a stellar NFL career.

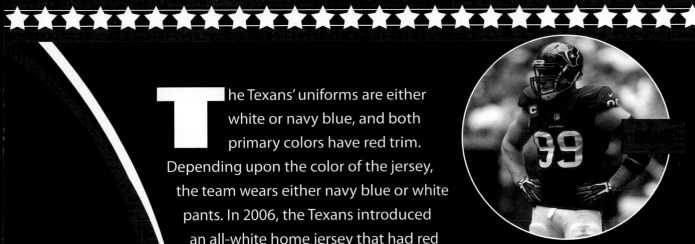

The Texans' uniforms are either white or navy blue, and both primary colors have red trim. Depending upon the color of the jersey, the team wears either navy blue or white pants. In 2006, the Texans introduced an all-white home jersey that had red numbers and blue trim.

The Texans have a number of **alternate jerseys**, the first of which is an all-blue jersey with white numbers and red trim, and the second of which is a red jersey with white pants. In 2007, the team premiered all-red jerseys with white numbers, blue trim, and red socks.

⊔ The Texans call it Battle Red Day when they wear their red jerseys at home. They encourage fans to also dress in red.

The Helmets

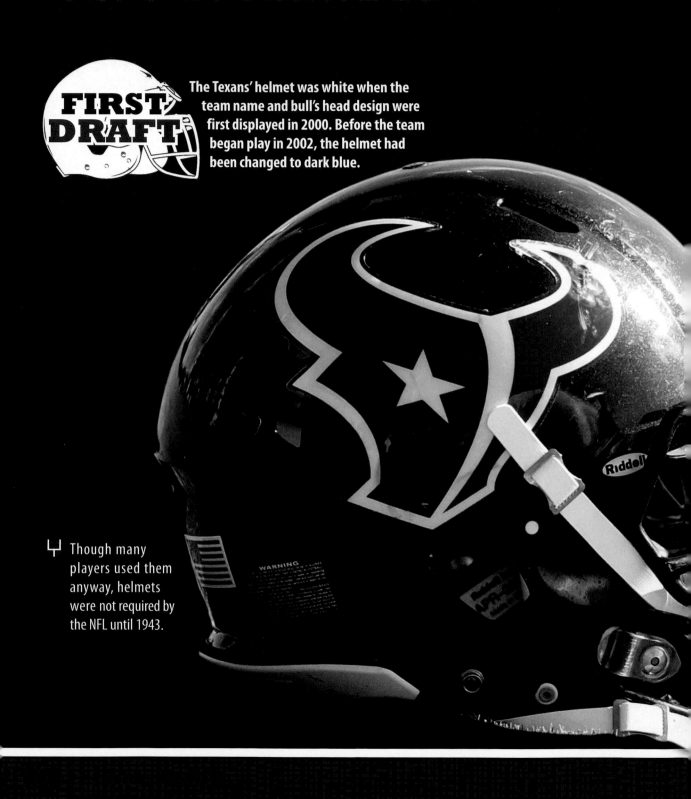

FIRST DRAFT

The Texans' helmet was white when the team name and bull's head design were first displayed in 2000. Before the team began play in 2002, the helmet had been changed to dark blue.

☐ Though many players used them anyway, helmets were not required by the NFL until 1943.

The Texans have only played in one helmet in their brief history. Owner Bob McNair described the colors of the Texans' helmet as "Deep Steel Blue," "Battle Red," and "Liberty White." The **logo** that adorns the helmet is an abstract bull's head. The bull's head logo is red and blue with white trim. A white line divides it into two halves in a manner intended to resemble the "**Lone Star**" flag of Texas.

Another shared characteristic between the flag of Texas and the helmet is the presence of the lone star itself, which appears in place of the bull's eye. Its five points are meant to represent pride, courage, strength, tradition, and independence. While the Texans have not been around the NFL quite long enough to have much in the way of tradition, their pride, courage, strength, and independence are on display on the football field every Sunday.

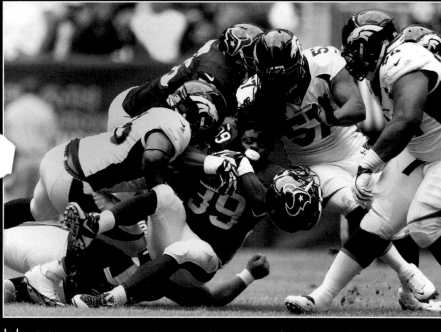

⬏ A helmet is so important during an NFL game that if a ball carrier loses his helmet, the play is considered over.

The Coaches

15 Bill O'Brien recorded 15 wins and 9 losses during his two seasons as Penn State's head coach.

⌐ In addition to being the head coach in Houston, Bill O'Brien will also serve as the team's offensive coordinator.

When the Texans started to search for their first head coach, they kept in mind the challenges of coaching a team that has no established leaders and no history. They chose veteran NFL coach Dom Capers. Having turned the expansion Carolina Panthers into Super Bowl contenders in just two seasons, Dom Capers had proven himself capable of handling the unique challenges presented to coaches of **expansion teams**.

DOM CAPERS

Dom Capers led the Carolina Panthers to an NFC Western Division title in the team's second year. He was said to work 17 hours per day and sleep on the couch in his office. Under Capers' guidance, the Texans improved in each of their first three seasons.

GARY KUBIAK

In Gary Kubiak's first seven seasons at the helm, the Texans climbed their way out of the AFC cellar and into the **postseason**. In 2012, they won a franchise-record 12 games and their second straight AFC South division title. The Texans were also among the top 10 NFL teams in both offense and defense.

BILL O'BRIEN

From 2007 to 2011, Bill O'Brien worked with the best in New England. As an assistant to Bill Belichick, and as Tom Brady's quarterback coach, O'Brien directed some of the best offenses in league history. Now the headman in Houston, O'Brien definitely has the resumé to lead a revival at NRG Stadium.

The Mascot

Toro's biography does not say how much he weighs, just that he is big enough to "bull" you over.

On April 21, 2001, the world witnessed the birth of Toro, a 6-foot-tall bull big enough to "bull you over." An athlete/scholar, Toro received his master's degree in acrobatics.

As a mascot for the Houston Texans, Toro displays his acrobatic skills every Sunday on the sideline, and sometimes performs stunts to amaze the crowd. Texans' fans have watched in awe as Toro has performed feats of daring such as zip lining upside-down across the playing field, and bungee jumping from the roof of NRG Stadium.

⌐ While Toro may be bull-sized, his shoe size is a modest 10 and a half.

⌐ Toro stays in shape by doing pushups after the Texans score.

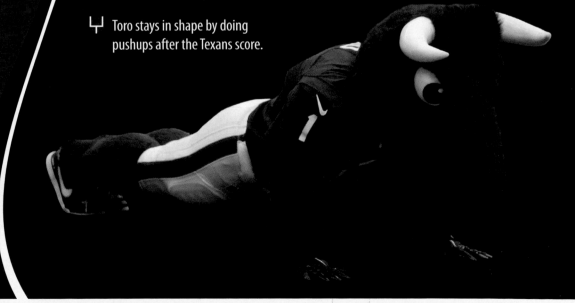

Legends of the Past

Many great players have suited up in the Texans' blue and red. A few of them have become icons of the team and the city it represents.

Dunta Robinson

A three-sport star in high school, Dunta Robinson excelled as a cornerback at the University of South Carolina. The Houston Texans drafted him with their first pick in the 2004 NFL Draft, and Robinson wasted no time in displaying his impressive skills.

In his rookie season with the Texans, Robinson intercepted six passes and made 87 tackles. Following that season, offenses became reluctant to throw the ball in Robinson's direction. However, he still managed to set a franchise record with 13 interceptions before leaving Houston in 2009.

Position Cornerback
Seasons 10 (2004–2013)
Born April 11, 1982, in Athens, Georgia

Mario Williams

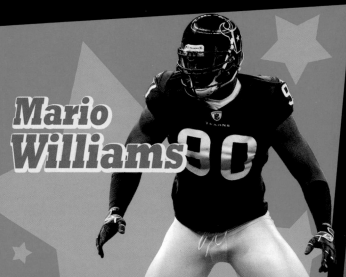

Position Defensive End
Seasons 8 (2006–2013)
Born January 31, 1985, in Richlands, North Carolina

Many people were critical when the Texans drafted defensive end Mario Williams over Reggie Bush and Vince Young in the 2006 NFL Draft. Those skeptics were proven foolish when Mario Williams became an **All-Pro** in just his second season in the league. In 2007, his 14 **sacks** accounted for 45 percent of the team's sack total and earned him the NFL Alumni Defensive Lineman of the Year award. While Williams's final two seasons with the Texans were marred by injury, he departed the team with the Texans' record for sacks (53) and forced fumbles (11).

Jason Babin

As a senior at Western Michigan University, Jason Babin recorded 115 tackles, 15 sacks, and 33 tackles behind the line of **scrimmage** and got the attention of many NFL teams. In the 2004 NFL Draft, the Texans traded a second-, third-, and fourth-round pick to the Tennessee Titans in exchange for the 27th pick overall. They used that pick to select the future two-time **Pro Bowler**. Babin's best season with the Texans may have been his rookie season, in which he started every game, amassed four sacks, 63 tackles, and defended two passes.

Position Linebacker-Defensive End
Seasons 10 (2004–2013)
Born May 24, 1980, in Kalamazoo, Michigan

DeMeco Ryans

In six years with Houston, DeMeco Ryans established himself as a tackling machine. An **All-American** with the University of Alabama, Ryans arrived in the NFL battle tested and ready to go. He didn't waste any time getting started. In his first professional season, Ryans registered 155 tackles, 3.5 sacks, intercepted a pass, recovered a fumble, and was named the Associated Press NFL Defensive Rookie of the Year.

In six years with the Texans, Ryans made two Pro Bowls and was named captain of the Texans' defense. Beloved for his professionalism and leadership, he earned the nickname "Cap'n Meco."

Position Linebacker
Seasons 8 (2006–2013)
Born July 28, 1984, in Bessemer, Alabama

Stars of Today

Today's Texans team is made up of many young, talented players who have proven that they are among the best players in the league.

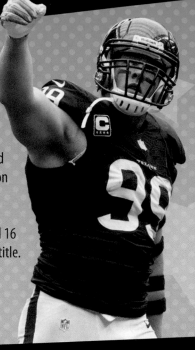

J. J. Watt

Coming out of high school, J. J. Watt was overlooked by many universities. As a college freshman, he was overlooked once again. It wasn't until Watt transferred to the University of Wisconsin that he began to attract attention. These days, the attention is not so hard to come by. In three years with the Texans, J. J. Watt emerged as one of the top defenders in the NFL. Following a promising rookie season, Watt exploded onto the national spotlight in 2012. He led the NFL with 20.5 sacks, forced four fumbles, deflected 16 passes, was named NFL Defensive Player of the Year, and carried the Texans to a division title.

Position Defensive End
Seasons 3 (2011–2013)
Born March 22, 1989, in Waukesha, Wisconsin

Brian Cushing

Utilizing his superior strength and excellent speed, Brian Cushing's rookie season was one to remember. He tied Ray Lewis for the AFC lead in tackles with 133, while racking up four sacks, 10 pass deflections, four interceptions, and two forced fumbles. Following a spectacular 2011 season, defensive coordinator Wade Phillips said of Cushing that he was "one of the best I've ever coached, and I've been at it a long time." Unfortunately, injuries limited Cushing's participation in the 2012 and 2013 seasons, but the Texans are confident that he will be a force for years to come.

Position Linebacker
Seasons 5 (2009–2013)
Born January 24, 1987, in Park Ridge, New Jersey

Andre Johnson

Andre Johnson is one of the greatest wide receivers of all time. His current average of 83 receiving yards per game is second on the NFL's all-time list. At his current pace, Johnson will crack the top 10 in career receiving yards by the end of the 2014 season. A former track and field star at the University of Miami, where he also to led the Hurricanes to a **Bowl Championship Series (BCS) National Championship** in 2002, Johnson holds eight different Texans' receiving records. He is the only player in NFL history to catch 60 or more passes in each of his first eight seasons.

Position Wide Receiver
Seasons 11 (2003–2013)
Born July 11, 1981, in Miami, Florida

Arian Foster

After a breakout junior season at the University of Tennessee, Arian Foster was convinced to stay on one more season. However, a new **offensive coordinator** meant a different role for Foster. Following a disappointing senior season, Foster signed as an undrafted **free agent** with the Houston Texans. Much of Foster's rookie season was spent on special teams, but he prepared diligently, awaiting his opportunity to prove what he could do. In his first start at running back, Foster gained 119 yards and scored two touchdowns on 20 carries. In his second season, he led the NFL in total rushing yards (1,616), rushing touchdowns (16), and rushing yards per game (101).

Position Running Back
Seasons 5 (2009–2013)
Born September 24, 1987, in Albuquerque, New Mexico

All-Time Records

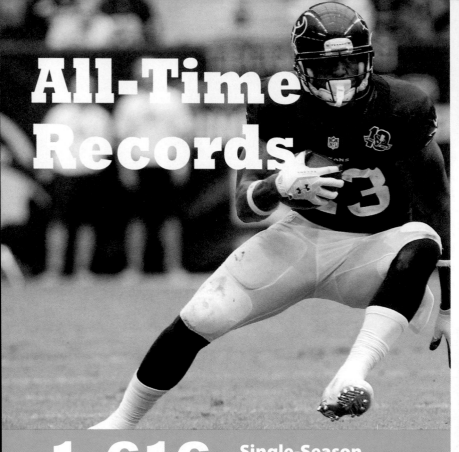

1,616 Single-Season Rushing Yards

In his first full season at running back, Arian Foster set the franchise's single-season mark for most rushing yards.

20.5 Single-Season Sacks

J. J. Watt's 20.5 sacks in 2012 led the NFL and set a Texans' single-season record. His 20.5 sacks were just two short of the NFL record.

482 Career Tackles

In six years with the Texans, DeMeco Ryans set the team record for tackles.

22,816

Career Passing Yards

With plenty of gas left in the tank, Matt Schaub hopes to build on his Texans' record for career passing yards.

1,598 Single-season Receiving Yards

Andre Johnson owns the top eight spots on the Texans' list for single-season receiving yards. He set the franchise record in 2012.

Timeline

Throughout the team's history, the Houston Texans have had many memorable events that have become defining moments for the team and its fans.

October 6, 1999
NFL owners vote 29-0 to award the newest expansion franchise to Houston and owner Bob McNair for $700 million.

2003
The Texans improve on their opening season by winning five regular-season games. Rookie receiver Andre Johnson catches 66 passes for 976 yards and Domanick Williams becomes the first Texan running back to rush for more than 1,000 yards.

In 2001, the Texans name Dom Capers as the franchise's first head coach.

| 1999 | 2000 | 2001 | 2002 | 2003 | 2004 |

2004
The Texans improve to a 7-9 win-loss record behind Pro Bowler Andre Johnson and David Carr's best season as a professional. However, a lack of consistency and a late-season loss to the hapless Cleveland Browns create concerns amongst Houston fans and ownership.

September 25, 2001
The Texans unveil their uniforms before an enthusiastic crowd of 12,000 football fans in downtown Houston.

September 8, 2002
The Texans open their first season with a home game at NRG Stadium against the Dallas Cowboys. They stage a huge upset, beating their intrastate rivals 19-10 and becoming the first expansion team to win their first game since the Minnesota Vikings in 1961.

April 29, 2006
In a stunning move, new head coach Gary Kubiak and Houston Texans' management select Mario Williams with the first pick in the 2006 NFL Draft. Many had expected the Texans to draft University of Southern California running back Reggie Bush or University of Texas quarterback Vince Young.

The Future
Although the Texans stumbled in 2013, Houston fans will expect a revival. The Texans are loaded with talent on both sides of the ball. The 2013 team had Super Bowl dreams that they were not able to fulfill. Although the Texans stumbled in 2013, Houston fans will expect a revival under new head coach Bill O'Brien.

In 2012, the Texans finish 12-4 and win their second consecutive AFC South division title.

2005	2007	2009	2011	2013	2015

In 2011, the Texans go 10-6 and win their first AFC South division title. Houston's defense improves from 29th in the league to fourth.

2007
In the Texans' first .500 season, Matt Schaub takes over the quarterbacking duties from David Carr and DeMeco Ryans continues his high level of play. Healthy and hungry to prove his worth, Mario Williams puts up star numbers, racking up 59 tackles and leading the Texans with 14 sacks.

January 12, 2013
One week after beating the Cincinnati Bengals in a rematch of the 2011 wild card game, the Texans face the New England Patriots in the divisional round of the playoffs. After falling behind 38-13, the Texans rally to cut the lead to 10 points. Unfortunately, they come up short, losing 41-28.

Write a Biography

Life Story

A person's life story can be the subject of a book. This kind of book is called a biography. Biographies often describe the lives of people who have achieved great success. These people may be alive today, or they may have lived many years ago. Reading a biography can help you learn more about a great person.

Get the Facts

Use this book, and research in the library and on the Internet, to find out more about your favorite Texan. Learn as much about this player as you can. What position does he play? What are his statistics in important categories? Has he set any records? Also, be sure to write down key events in the person's life. What was his childhood like? What has he accomplished off the field? Is there anything else that makes this person special or unusual?

Use the Concept Web

A concept web is a useful research tool. Read the questions in the concept web on the following page. Answer the questions in your notebook. Your answers will help you write a biography.

Concept Web

Adulthood
- Where does this individual currently reside?
- Does he or she have a family?

Your Opinion
- What did you learn from the books you read in your research?
- Would you suggest these books to others?
- Was anything missing from these books?

Childhood
- Where and when was this person born?
- Describe his or her parents, siblings, and friends.
- Did this person grow up in unusual circumstances?

Accomplishments off the Field
- What is this person's life's work?
- Has he or she received awards or recognition for accomplishments?
- How have this person's accomplishments served others?

Write a Biography

Help and Obstacles
- Did this individual have a positive attitude?
- Did he or she receive help from others?
- Did this person have a mentor?
- Did this person face any hardships?
- If so, how were the hardships overcome?

Accomplishments on the Field
- What records does this person hold?
- What key games and plays have defined his or her career?
- What are his or her stats in categories important to his or her position?

Work and Preparation
- What was this person's education?
- What was his or her work experience?
- How does this person work; what is the process he or she uses?

Trivia Time

Take this quiz to test your knowledge of the Houston Texans.
The answers are printed upside-down under each question.

1 How many times have the Houston Texans qualified for the postseason?

A. Two

2 Who is the Houston Texans all-time leader in passing yards?

A. Matt Schaub

3 Who coached the Houston Texans to back-to-back playoff appearances in 2011 and 2012?

A. Gary Kubiak

4 Who is the Texans' single-game and single-season rushing record holder?

A. Arian Foster

5 Which Texans' wide receiver holds the team record for single-season and career receiving yards?

A. Andre Johnson

6 How many helmet designs have the Houston Texans actually used during a game?

A. One

7 Which Texans' linebacker finished tied for the AFC lead in tackles in his rookie season?

A. Brian Cushing

8 Who is the Texans' all-time sacks leader?

A. Mario Williams

9 In what season did the Houston Texans win their first AFC South Division title?

A. 2011

10 What do the five points of Houston's "Lone Star" represent?

A. pride, courage, strength, tradition, and independence

Key Words

.500 season: when a team wins and loses an equal number of games. In the NFL, an 8-8 win-loss record is a .500 season

All-American: a player, usually in high school or college, judged to be the best in each position of a sport

All-Pro: an NFL player judged to be the best in his position for a given season

alternate jerseys: a jersey that sports teams may wear in games instead of their home or away uniforms

Bowl Championship Series (BCS) National Championship: an arrangement of five American college postseason football games to determine the national champion

expansion teams: brand new teams in a sports league, usually from cities that have not hosted a team in that league before

free agent: a player who is not currently under contract to play with a particular team

logo: a symbol that stands for a team or organization

Lone Star: a picture of a single star that the Houston Texans use in their logo design

offensive coordinator: a coaching staff member of a gridiron football team who is in charge of the offense

playoffs: the games played following the end of the regular season; six teams qualify: the four winners of the different conferences, and the two best teams that did not finish first in their conference, called the wild cards

postseason: a sporting event that takes place after the end of the regular season

Pro Bowler: NFL players who take part in the annual all-star game that pits the best players in the National Football Conference against the best players in the American Football Conference

retractable roof: a roof that can move to from an open position into a closed or extended position that completely covers the field of play and spectator areas

sacks: a sack occurs when the quarterback is tackled behind the line of scrimmage before he can throw a forward pass

scrimmage: the yard-line on the field from which the play starts

Super Bowl: the NFL's annual championship game between the winning team from the NFC and the winning team from the AFC

Index

Log on to www.av2books.com

AV[2] by Weigl brings you media enhanced books that support active learning. Go to www.av2books.com, and enter the special code found on page 2 of this book. You will gain access to enriched and enhanced content that supplements and complements this book. Content includes video, audio, weblinks, quizzes, a slide show, and activities.

AV[2] Online Navigation

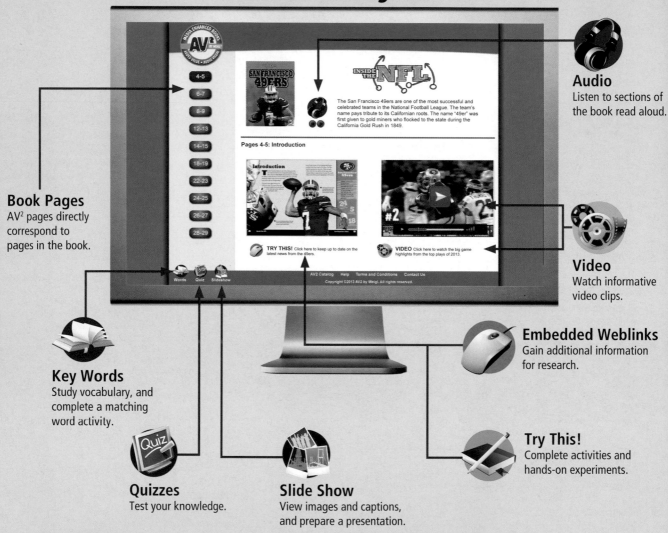

Book Pages
AV[2] pages directly correspond to pages in the book.

Audio
Listen to sections of the book read aloud.

Video
Watch informative video clips.

Key Words
Study vocabulary, and complete a matching word activity.

Embedded Weblinks
Gain additional information for research.

Quizzes
Test your knowledge.

Slide Show
View images and captions, and prepare a presentation.

Try This!
Complete activities and hands-on experiments.

AV[2] was built to bridge the gap between print and digital. We encourage you to tell us what you like and what you want to see in the future.

Sign up to be an AV[2] Ambassador at www.av2books.com/ambassador.